Original title:
Humorous Hickories

Copyright © 2025 Creative Arts Management OÜ
All rights reserved.

Author: Nathaniel Blackwood
ISBN HARDBACK: 978-1-80567-416-0
ISBN PAPERBACK: 978-1-80567-715-4

The Chuckling Comfrey Chronicles

In a garden so grand, where the oddballs grow,
The flowers tell tales that only they know.
With petal-shaped hats and roots that can dance,
They giggle through evenings, given half a chance.

The carrots wear glasses, quite thick and round,
They squint at the onions, who cry on the ground.
The tomatoes are blushing, quite red in the face,
While radishes chuckle, it's quite the odd place.

A dandelion's joke leaves the daisies in tears,
As the sunflowers wobble and skip in their gears.
The spinach is cracking up, rolling with laughter,
While the zucchini twirls, hoping for ever after.

At night, when the moon slicks the path with a glow,
The herbs come together, all ready for show.
With costumes and stories of their silly plight,
They dance in the moonlight, a whimsical sight.

Laughter in the Leaves

In the branches, jokes abound,
Squirrels chitter, making sound.
The acorns fall, a clumsy dance,
Nature's jesters, not a chance.

Owl hoots with a wink so sly,
As the moon begins to pry.
Giggles rise from bushes near,
Whispers tickle, spread the cheer.

Chuckles by the Creek

Bubbling water, sings a tune,
Frogs jump high, they're quite a boon.
Ducklings waddle, what a sight,
Quacking jokes, their hearts so light.

Turtles chuckle, sit and bask,
In this joy, they need no mask.
Fish leap up, then splash away,
Making ripples in dismay.

Mirth Among the Maples

Maple leaves like laughter dance,
In the breeze, they sway and prance.
Bees hum tunes of silly rhymes,
Buzzing softly, wasting time.

A chipmunk trips near roots of gold,
Tells a tale, humorous, bold.
Foliage rustles in delight,
Nature's comedy takes flight.

Giggles in the Glade

In the glade, where shadows play,
Breezes stir the leaves in sway.
Ladybugs in polka dots,
Join the laughter, tying knots.

Bunnies hop with silly flair,
Poking fun, without a care.
In the glade, all troubles cease,
Each smile shared, a bit of peace.

Folly Among the Ferns

In the glade where laughter blooms,
A squirrel donned a pair of looms.
He stitched a vest, bright green and bold,
Jumping jacks for tales retold.

A frog in bowtie took a leap,
Claiming he's the king, not sheep.
Amidst the leaves, a dance of grace,
With twinkling eyes, he's running the race.

Jestful Journeys in the Juniper

A raccoon with a map in hand,
Declared he'd travel to a distant land.
But tripped on roots, his plans were foiled,
In giggles soft, the forest boiled.

The owl, with spectacles, did squint,
As tales of mishaps made him grin.
"Dear raccoon, path-finder of plight,
You're better suited for a night-light."

Riddles of the Redwood

Tall trees whispered secret games,
Of knock-knock jokes and silly names.
With branches bent in hello cheer,
They tickled tales for all to hear.

A chipmunk dressed in stripes of brown,
Joked he'd won the best-dressed crown.
While shadows stretched and caught the glare,
He danced with zest, a little rare.

Snickers in the Sycamores

In sycamores where giggles sprout,
A raccoon danced and spun about.
Chasing shadows, he missed a beat,
Fell into leaves at the raccoon's feet.

The stars above twinkled with glee,
As the crew erupted, wild and free.
With every twist and playful shove,
Nature smiled, and so did love.

The Laughing Willow

In a grove where giggles bloom,
The willow sways with thoughts of doom.
Its branches droop in playful jest,
While squirrels dance, all dressed the best.

With whispers soft, it tells a joke,
The rabbits roll, they nearly choke.
A breeze plays tricks, the leaves all flap,
"Watch out for sneezes!" warns a chap.

A crow swoops down with feathers bright,
To join the fun from morning light.
It caws a tune, a silly song,
As all the creatures sing along.

So if you pass that laughing tree,
You'll find a show, just wait and see.
In nature's laugh, the joy is clear,
Planting moments full of cheer.

Acorn Antics and Silly Tales

Acorns tumble, what a sight,
Racing down, oh what delight!
Squirrels chase with frantic feet,
Join the fun, it can't be beat.

A daring nut rolls down a hill,
Creating chaos, oh what thrill!
The chipmunks giggle, tails in air,
As everyone laughs without a care.

In the shade, the stories flow,
Of nutty nights and silly shows.
The trees shake laughter from their leaves,
As playful winds weave through the eaves.

This woodland realm holds many dreams,
With acorn capers and silly schemes.
So come and share a chuckle or two,
In this jolly place, there's fun for you.

Pinecone Puns and Shenanigans

Pinecones tumble, spin, and roll,
Creating laughter as their goal.
They bounce around, a merry bunch,
While creatures watch and laugh a hunch.

A wise old owl gives a cheer,
"These pinecone puns are top-notch here!"
A hedgehog snickers, quills all spiked,
As everyone joins, the mood gets hiked.

Each pinecone holds a little joke,
A secret laugh beneath the oak.
With every joke, there's joy that's sent,
In nature's play, all sorrows bent.

So gather round and join the fun,
These pinecone tales are never done.
With chuckles shared through forest trails,
You'll find the joy in leafy gales.

Follies in the Forest

In the forest where mischief thrives,
The critters dance, all joy survives.
A dance-off starts 'neath moonlit beams,
With twirling tails and silly dreams.

The rabbits hop and the fox joins in,
While deer are laughing, what a win!
Every sound is filled with glee,
From chirping birds to buzzing bee.

The trees all sway to this grand tune,
As squirrels gather nuts, a bustling boon.
With every folly and frolic spree,
This forest bursts with jubilee.

So if you wander through these woods,
Join every step, just knock on wood.
For in this place of playful cheer,
Follies bloom throughout the year.

Witty Whispers of the Wilderness

In the woods where creatures play,
Squirrels dance and chipmunks sway,
A raccoon wears the autumn's hat,
While badgers giggle, 'Look at that!'

The owls hoot a cheeky tune,
While frogs croak under the moon,
A deer does yoga, strikes a pose,
While pine trees whisper all their woes.

Clumsy Critters in the Canopy

Monkeys swing, then fall in stacks,
Bouncing off their buddy's backs,
A parrot laughs, 'You're such a klutz!'
As they tumble through tree trunks and ruts.

Sloths hang out, they hardly move,
Until one shimmies, makes a groove,
The others cheer like rowdy fans,
While ants march by with colorful plans.

The Guffaws of the Great Blue Heron

A heron stands, all poised and grand,
With one webbed foot in a puddle of sand,
He wobbles, tilts, and starts to sway,
Catching fish in a clumsy way.

As frogs jump round, they can't believe,
This elegant bird's prime-time reprieve,
He shakes his feathers, strikes a pose,
Then slips right in—oh how it goes!

Barking Mad and Other Silliness

A dog in a hat, such a sight to see,
Barks at the moon with all his glee,
A cat rolls by, gives a sideways glance,
And starts plotting an elegant dance.

The trees seem to laugh with a rustling sound,
As branches sway up and down all around,
A picnic table springs to life,
Juggling watermelons, a fruit-filled strife!

Whims and Whispers Under the Willows

Beneath the willows, shadows dance,
A squirrel twirls in fancy pants.
A frog croaks jokes, a witty chap,
While the breeze giggles, oh what a flap.

The sun peeks through with a cheeky grin,
As birds gossip, let the fun begin.
A bumblebee buzzes, it's quite a cheer,
As nature joins in, everyone's near.

The rabbit hops with a surprise twist,
While fireflies light up the evening mist.
A joyful symphony shapes the air,
With laughter echoing everywhere.

Beneath the willows, laughter grows,
In this playful grove, anything goes.
So come and share in this mirthful place,
Where smiles and chuckles adorn each face.

The Zany Zelkova Adventures

Under the zelkova, wild and free,
A raccoon struts with zestful glee.
He flips and flops, making quite a scene,
In this leafy realm, joy's evergreen.

A parrot squawks, recounting a tale,
Of the time a squirrel rode a snail.
With every twist, the laughter grows,
In the realm where the zelkova glows.

A troupe of ants, in marching band,
Play tiny drums, so grandly planned.
They parade through roots, what a delight,
Turning the day into a funny sight.

From silly pranks to dances bright,
The zelkova hums, a pure delight.
With every breeze, more stories unfold,
In this zany haven, laughter is gold.

Chuckling at the Cottonwood

In the cottonwood's sway, the whims take flight,
A dandelion wishes with all its might.
A chipmunk juggles acorns with flair,
While crickets chime in, a musical air.

The wind nudges gently, tickling leaves,
As laughter erupts where mischief deceives.
A family of squirrels in a friendly race,
Chasing shadows, full of embrace.

A turtle pokes out, a curious sight,
Wearing a cap, oh what a delight!
He tells his tales, each one a surprise,
Bringing wide smiles and brightening eyes.

Under the cottonwood, all troubles cease,
As giggles abound, a moment's peace.
So join the fun under branches wide,
Where chuckles and joy are the ultimate guide.

Two Treetop Turtles Tell Tales

In the treetops high, two turtles convene,
With shells for seats, they're quite the scene.
They share wild stories of daring quests,
Of mischief and joy, their laughter rests.

One turtle claims he jumped a tall tree,
While the other shakes his head, full of glee.
They throw in puns, each funnier than the last,
With echoes of chuckles, their moments amassed.

A breeze carries laughter, as they compete,
Over who can grasp the silliest feat.
Between the branches, tales soar and glide,
As the treetop turtles with laughter abide.

In this leafy realm, friendship takes flight,
Their antics spread cheer, from day into night.
So listen closely to their merry chatter,
For in treetops, joy's the only matter.

Guffaws in the Greenery

In the woods where laughter grows,
Bushes giggle, no one knows.
Squirrels dance on branches high,
Tickle the leaves, a sprightly sigh.

Frogs wear hats, jump to the beat,
Chirping crickets play their fleet.
Dancing flowers twirl and sway,
Join the fun in their own way.

Bunnies bounce with fluffy glee,
Winking at the big old tree.
A rustling breeze, a playful tease,
Nature's jesters aim to please.

If you listen, you can hear,
Whispers of joy, full of cheer.
Every twig and twiggy friend,
Raising smiles that never end.

Pranks of the Pine Needles

Underneath the tall, green spires,
Pine needles play the best of liars.
One sneaks up to tickle toes,
As another giggles, nobody knows.

Branches stretch with teasing flair,
Sprinkling laughter in the air.
An acorn drops with a whacky plop,
Sending giggles all around, nonstop.

Sappy jokes drip from the bark,
Blowing kisses like a spark.
Rustling pine cones roll and spin,
In this forest, fun's a win.

Woodpeckers knock, a silly song,
Nature's rhythm, light and strong.
Pranks abound from tree to crest,
In this woodland, we jest the best.

Satirical Sunbeams

The sun up high has quite the grin,
Winking rays spark joy within.
Clouds giggle as they float on by,
Playing peek-a-boo with the sky.

Shadows stretch with a twisty dance,
Making silly shapes that prance.
A lazy dog rolls in delight,
Grinning wide at the sun's bright light.

Butterflies flaunt their patterned wear,
Teasing blooms with flirty air.
Each petal laughs, a floral jest,
In the glow of rays, all is blessed.

Sunbeams bounce like children free,
Chasing shadows beneath each tree.
Nature's grin is wide and bold,
In this warm light, be joyful, be told!

The Comic Canopy

A canopy of laughter, how it glows,
Branches burst with giggly prose.
Witty vines weave tight and snug,
Creating puns like a cozy hug.

Raccoons plot with tiny tricks,
Hoping to snag a treat for kicks.
Wise old owls chuckle as they see,
The playful antics of every tree.

Lemonade streams flow with zest,
While woodland critters take a rest.
Under the boughs, jokes are spun,
In this land of laughter, we've just begun.

Swaying grass joins the harmony,
Swaying lightly, feeling free.
Nature's stage, and all who play,
Make the world a cheerful array.

The Joyful Jumble of Jargon

In a town where words just play,
Silly phrases dance all day.
A button's blue, a feather's green,
The quirkiest sights you've ever seen.

A pickle sings, a shoe runs fast,
In this odd place, nothing's steadfast.
Balloons speak truths that never lie,
While cats debate the whys and why.

No need for sense, just laugh aloud,
Join the gibberish, be proud.
When logic leaves, hilarity calls,
In this jumble, joy befalls.

Whimsical Whispers of the Wilderness

The trees conspire, they chuckle soft,
As leaves take flight, aloft, aloft.
A rabbit juggles acorns with glee,
While squirrels plot their next jubilee.

The brook hums tunes of a froggy song,
Where turtles march, they feel so strong.
A feathered choir, all out of tune,
Sings to the rhythm of the bright full moon.

In this wooded laugh, the critters sway,
Where nonsense reigns in a merry play.
A picnic of giggles under the sky,
Join in the mirth, oh my, oh my!

Barking Up the Wrong Trees

Oh, the pup thinks the branch is grand,
Wagging his tail in a goofy stand.
But up in the crook, there's a curious cat,
Looking down puzzled at the doggy's spat.

The owl rolls eyes at the fuss below,
While the squirrel giggles, stealing the show.
A wise old crow caws with delight,
As chaos blooms under the moonlight.

They bark, they squawk, what a wild scene,
In the forest where nonsense reigns supreme.
A game of chase, a bark or a two,
In the merry woods, it's all so askew.

A Squirrel's Misadventures

A squirrel woke up with quite the plan,
To gather more nuts than any man.
He dashed through the grass, a whirl of fuzz,
With dreams of feasts and endless buzz.

But oh, what a blunder, into a pool,
He splashed and slipped, looked quite the fool.
With acorns floating like boats set free,
He paddled with paws, what absurdity!

On the tree he'd climb, then slide right down,
His fluffy tail pats his funny frown.
He teeters and totters, what a sight!
In his wacky world, all feels just right.

Nutty Narratives from the Nature Patch

There once was a squirrel with big dreams,
He wore a top hat and danced by the streams.
But when he twirled, he slipped on a nut,
And landed smack-dab in a raccoon's butt.

The raccoon just laughed, said, "You're quite the star!"
As he took a selfie, oh my, look how bizarre!
They joined a parade with frogs wearing crowns,
In a wacky town where nobody frowns.

A woodpecker drummed to a funky beat,
While a rabbit breakdanced on tiny feet.
The mushrooms all cheered, in colors so bright,
As the forest lit up with pure delight.

When evening fell, they'd gather for tales,
Of mishaps and giggles, of magical gales.
Under the moon, with a wink and a nod,
Laughter echoed, oh what a façade!

The Enchanted Elderberry Escapades

In a bush of berries, a bear took a seat,
Declaring, "I'm berry-full, let's make this a treat!"
His friends rolled in, a raccoon and a goat,
They planned a grand feast on a floating boat.

The goat brought some hay, the raccoon some pie,
While the bear spread jelly and asked, "Oh my!"
They chased all the butterflies around the lake,
Only to find they were stuck in a cake.

With giggles and gaffes, they danced in a line,
The elderberries wobbled, saying, "Oh, that's divine!"
A wise old owl hooted from up in a tree,
"These elderberry shenanigans are key to glee!"

When the sun dipped low, they raised tiny cups,
Filled with juice from the berries, for friendship it tops.
Under starlit skies with laughter so loud,
They danced and they feasted, a jubilant crowd!

The Collapsing Cedar Comedy Club

In a cedar tree tall, the jokes went to town,
With a raccoon as host and a bear in a gown.
They stacked up some acorns for seats all around,
And promised a laugh with each joke that they found.

An owl told a story that got everyone giggly,
While a chipmunk dressed up and danced all wiggly.
A squirrel with a pun tossed a nut in the air,
"I can't handle all this! I think I need air!"

The crowd roared with laughter as pinecones would fall,
As the antics grew louder, they'd rise and enthrall.
"Tell me, dear bear, does this outfit look fine?"
"Only if you promise to share some of mine!"

As night came to call, the laughter still thrived,
With memories of giggles, the forest felt alive.
In trees wide and tall, where humor ran deep,
They whispered the secrets that night they would keep!

Fabled Folly of Forest Friends

In a glade full of stories, the friends gathered round,
Where laughter and folly together were found.
A fox made a wager that he could outsmart,
A turtle in chess with a very quick start.

The turtle just smiled, all calm and composed,
While the fox pranced about, overly imposed.
With each graceful move, the fox seemed to clown,
But lost every round, and the crowd laughed him down.

A beaver then joined with a stack of some logs,
He built up a bridge that connected to frogs.
With leaps and with croaks, they danced in delight,
As the humor unfolded beneath the moonlight.

As the night wore on, tales were spun with cheer,
Echoes of giggles could be heard far and near.
In the heart of the woods, where friendships take flight,
The folly of forest friends brought pure starlight!

Funny Business in the Birch Buds

In the woods where the birch trees sway,
A squirrel dressed up in a bright ballet.
He twirled and leaped, causing quite a scene,
While the rabbits stared, looking rather keen.

The owls hooted loud, a curious bunch,
As the porcupines gathered for a brunch.
They sipped on dew from the leaves above,
Proclaiming it was the soup of love.

A chipmunk with glasses read stories with flair,
To an audience of critters, all sitting there.
He stumbled on words, caused a fit of grin,
And the raccoons laughed, trying not to spin.

So if you wander where the birch trees play,
Expect some antics to brighten your day.

Laughing Leaves and Other Nonsense

In the garden where the silly leaves dance,
A beetle in boots tried to break into prance.
He slipped on a petal, oh what a sight,
While ladybugs giggled at his silly plight.

A worm with a hat proclaimed himself king,
He ruled over flowers, demanding a swing.
But lavender insisted, they now just want tea,
With cookies for critters, oh what glee!

The wind joined the fun, whistled a tune,
While sunflowers stretched, swaying like a loon.
They chuckled and chuckled, a sight so absurd,
As a butterfly landed, never deterred.

So if you stroll where the laughter is loud,
Join in with the leaves, you'll feel so proud.

The Silly Sycamore Saga

At the heart of the field stood a sycamore,
With branches that waved and a trunk that could roar.
It tickled the clouds and whispered the ground,
Creating a racket, a joy that profound.

Two raccoons in tuxedos planned a grand feast,\nWhile
the tree played host, booming the least.
They danced around roots, served acorns with glee,
And invited the bunnies—'Come eat with me!'

A fox with a grin joined the spree without fright,
Juggled three apples, a marvelous sight.
But one took a dive, splashed right in the brook,
Sending a splash that made all creatures look.

From that day forth, in the sycamore's shade,
Many laughed loudly, their worries allayed.

Fumbles in the Field

In the field where the daisies twirl and play,
A clumsy old moose fumbled on his way.
He tripped on a rock, landed with a thud,
And laughed at himself, covered in mud.

The frogs croaked a tune, cheering him on,
While a sheep in a scarf yawned, blinked at the dawn.
They spun tales of mishaps, of moments gone wrong,
With giggles and snorts, they all sang along.

A hedgehog in glasses misread the sign,
And wandered in circles, claiming it's fine.
The others just chuckled, "Oh dear friend of ours,
Trust us, it's noon and not the dark hours!"

So if you're in fields, let your laughter flow,
Join the fun of the fumbles—it's a wild show!

Laugh Lines in the Landscape

In the meadow where daisies sway,
Butterflies giggle, oh what a day!
The squirrels wear hats made of leaves,
Telling tall tales to the busy bees.

The old oak tree chuckles so loud,
As the rabbits hop, feeling quite proud.
With each passing cloud, they all have fun,
Dancing and prancing under the sun.

The grass whispers jokes to the breeze,
As crickets play songs with such ease.
A chorus of laughter fills the air,
Nature's comedy show, beyond compare!

So come join the fun, don't be shy,
Laugh with the flowers and watch time fly.
In this world where giggles grow,
The landscape's alive and steals the show.

Cheery Chats with Chipmunks

In the shade of a great big pine,
Chipmunks gather, oh how they shine!
Chit-chatting 'bout their latest snacks,
With acorns and berries filling their packs.

One wears a vest, so dapper and neat,
While another juggles twigs with his feet.
"Hey, did you hear about the owl's new tie?"
"It's purple with polka dots, oh my oh my!"

They gossip and giggle under the sun,
Making the forest a place full of fun.
With each little pun, their cheeks round and bright,
The chipmunks bring laughter, pure delight!

So if you stroll through the woods one day,
Listen closely to what they say.
For in their chatter, joy will you'll find,
A comedy club of the chipmunk kind!

Amusing Anecdotes of the Ailanthus

The mighty tree sways, proud and tall,
Sharing silly stories with creatures in thrall.
"Once had a leaf that danced in the rain,
Claimed it was going to a leaf-ball again!"

A bird chirps in, "Oh please, can't you see?
That leaf was just laughing at you and me!"
The branches shake, and the laughter does spread,
As the ailanthus shakes off its leafy dread.

A butterfly flits, with a grin on her face,
"Tell us again about your trunk's big race!"
"Faster than lightning, I took to the air,
Dodged pesky bugs with flair and a dare!"

All the critters gather 'round, hearts so light,
As the tree tells its tales from morning till night.
With each new hoot, each giggle, each cheer,
The ailanthus spreads joy loud and clear!

Nonsense in the Nook

In a cozy nook where the shadows play,
A hedgehog spins yarns in his funny way.
"Once I wore shoes, oh what a sight!
Danced with a cat in the pale moonlight!"

The flowers lean in to hear each tall tale,
As bumblebees join in, buzzing without fail.
"A frog tried to sing, but oh what a mess!
His notes were so high, it caused quite the stress!"

A raccoon pokes in, a grin on his face,
"Tell us the one 'bout the snail and the race!"
"He zoomed so fast, but tripped on his shell,
And ended up stuck in a sticky old well!"

So gather around, let the hilarity flow,
In that little nook where the wild things roam.
With laughter aplenty and nonsense galore,
The fun never stops; there's always more!

The Whimsical Woods

In a forest where the trees wear hats,
Squirrels dance like chubby little brats.
The owls hoot jokes, oh so absurd,
And butterflies giggle, not saying a word.

The rivers chuckle, splashing with glee,
While raccoons play chess under an old pine tree.
Each branch holds a laugh, each leaf a wisecrack,
As nature's own comedians keep the fun on track.

Beneath the tall oaks with their wobbly bark,
There's a party of critters, all jumping at dark.
The moon shines a spotlight on antics so bright,
With laughter and frolicking, oh, what a sight!

So if you wander where the silly trees grow,
Expect all the giggles and jesting in tow.
For in this whimsical wood, full of cheer,
Every rustle and whisper brings joy far and near.

Jests in the Jamboree

At the jamboree, the toads wear their coats,
While frogs trade tall tales and add silly quotes.
The crickets play music with tiny violins,
As the raccoons judge, amid laughter and spins.

Balloons tied to branches float high in the air,
While owls wear party hats, spinning round without care.
The party is lively, with snacks made of mud,
And everyone's dancing, all covered in crud.

A chipmunk shows off his latest dance move,
The crowd erupts loudly, they all start to groove.
With cookies and giggles piled higher than hills,
Each nibbled delight brings uproarious thrills!

So join in the fun, bring your silliest grin,
For this jamboree chaos is where it begins.
With jesters and joy from the start to the end,
You'll leave with a smile, a new woodland friend!

The Quirky Quercus

Under the quirky oak with its twisty old limbs,
The squirrels tell tales of their daring whims.
They race up the trunk, all while making yaps,
Beware of their acorns, they fall with loud slaps!

With branches that wiggle and leaves that shake,
This tree's got a talent, make no mistake!
A parrot named Pete, with a flair for the cheek,
Mocks the old fox who's aging and weak.

Dancing around the roots, the rabbits all cheer,
Each hop comes with giggles, oh, lend me your ear!
For the tales from the Quercus are simply the best,
A portrait of laughter right here in the nest.

So if you feel weary, come play in the shade,
Find joy in the antics, be not dismayed.
For with every rustling leaf and joke shared,
The quirky old oak shows how much it cared!

Silliness in the Saplings

In the field of young saplings, where laughter abounds,
Tiny creatures skitter with gusts of sweet sounds.
A caterpillar races a snail with a grin,
While ladybugs cheer them, both cheering to win!

The sunflowers sway like they're dancing in line,
As bees buzz their tunes, oh, how they entwine!
Each petal a puppet in this lively show,
The giggles and glee continue to flow.

A hedgehog brings snacks that are truly a feast,
While ants tell tall tales of their biggest beast.
Together they share in the silliness bright,
As the day fades to dusk with a soft, glowing light.

So come to the saplings where mirth never ends,
Join the playful antics and make lots of friends.
In the heart of the meadow, where joy's always sown,
You'll find the sweet laughter that feels like home.

Giggling in the Grove

In the grove where the squirrels play,
Acorns bounce like they own the day.
A raccoon wears a hat too wide,
Doing a jig with a silly slide.

The trees laugh as the branches sway,
Funny critters in a grand display.
A bunny hops with a floppy ear,
Causing giggles for all to hear.

A woodpecker taps to a bouncy beat,
While frogs jump high in a goofy feat.
The sun peeks through the leaves all bright,
As laughter fills the afternoon light.

So come and join the merry crowd,
In the grove where joy is loud.
Nature holds a festival spree,
With giggles shared in harmony.

The Whimsical Woodshed

In the woodshed, tools have a chat,
A saw and a hammer picked up a spat.
The tape measure stretched out so long,
Claims it can dance to a funky song.

A squirrel snickers at a rusty nail,
While paint cans gossip without fail.
A ladder leans with an elegant flair,
As the rakes gossip about who has hair.

A woodpile laughs, stacking its height,
While the lantern glows deep into night.
They tell tall tales of projects past,
Hoping the laughter, forever will last.

So step right in and join the jest,
In the woodshed, it's simply the best.
With tools that chatter, and stories to spread,
You'll leave with a smile, and jokes in your head.

Treetop Tickle Fest

In the treetops, a tickle fight,
With branches waving, what a sight!
The owls hoot with giggly glee,
As squirrels giggle from each tree.

Leaves are tickling the blossoms bright,
Dancing together in sheer delight.
A chipmunk squeaks, 'What a grand time!'
Still munching on acorns, which is sublime!

A parrot cackles from way up high,
Spreading laughter as it learns to fly.
They swing and sway in the gentle breeze,
Sharing secrets like old buddies with ease.

So high above, the fun will last,
In a tickle fest, joy unsurpassed.
With nature's laughter echoing free,
The treetops sing in sweet harmony.

Tall Tales of the Timberlands

In timberlands where stories grow,
Tall tales twist in a funny flow.
A bear tells of stealing a pie,
While the rabbit winks and rolls an eye.

The deer prances with a comic flair,
Claiming it danced with the market fair.
The hedgehogs giggle as they discuss
Why their spines are a fashionable plus.

A fox spins yarns of sneaky plans,
While bees buzz back with little jabs and pans.
The trees sway, shaking their heads,
As laughter echoes, filling the threads.

So gather round, hear stories bold,
Of critters and fun that never grow old.
In the timberlands, let joy prevail,
With chuckles and grins in every tale.

The Great Nutty Race

Squirrels in their tiny cars,
Revved up beneath the stars.
Chasing acorns, what a sight,
Zooming left and zooming right.

Over bumps and through the grass,
Pine cones fly as they all pass.
Laughter echoes, fur ablaze,
Squirrelly antics in a craze.

With a twist, one took a spill,
Rolling down with endless thrill.
Nutty chaos, pure delight,
In this race, all hearts feel light.

Who knew nature could be fun?
Underneath the warming sun.
The victor swings from branch to tree,
In nutty races, joy runs free.

A Prankster's Pine Adventure

In a forest full of giggles,
A crafty pine tree snickers and wiggles.
Hiding acorns, placing pranks,
Leaving critters in silly, fun banks.

A raccoon slips on a slimy log,
While a deer jumps up, startled in fog.
The pine tree laughs, sways tall and wide,
As laughter bubbles from side to side.

Chasing shadows, what a game,
Each creature's antics just the same.
The woodland's full of jests and glee,
In the heart of this tree, pure jubilee.

As the moon rises with a grin,
Pranks continue, nature's din.
A night of jest, the stars do twinkle,
In the pranking woods, hearts do crinkle.

Jovial Journeys of the Juniper

Junipers with giggles swayed,
On grassy paths, adventures laid.
With every twist and every turn,
Laughter blooms like fires that burn.

A gopher rides on a toadstool throne,
While mischievous owls hoot quite alone.
With tales of fortune and silly tricks,
They weave a tapestry that quickly flicks.

Pair of rabbits hop and prance,
In this joyful woodland dance.
Chasing tails without a care,
Each journey bursting, humor to share.

Through the bushes and under the sun,
Their jovial journeys have just begun.
In a land where giggles never cease,
Junipers spread happiness like a lease.

Ticklish Twigs and Happy Tails

Ticklish twigs intertwined in glee,
As squirrels play and climb up a tree.
With happy tails waving high,
They dart and prance, oh my, oh my!

A chipmunk squeaks, a thistle's stuck,
While others laugh, oh what bad luck!
Branches sway with laughter's song,
In this woodland, they all belong.

Belly laughs from feathered friends,
In a game that never ends.
Chasing shadows, making noise,
In the forest, pure joy deploys.

As dusk descends and stars appear,
The ticklish twigs still hold their cheer.
In the heart of nature, laughter trails,
Creating stories, joy prevails.

Raccoon Revelry at Twilight

In the dusk of the yard, where shadows leap,
Raccoons breakdance, not a soul asleep.
They tip over bins, with a flick and a twist,
Charms of the night, too fun to resist.

With masks on their faces, they steal a few fries,
Planning their chaos under moonlit skies.
They chatter and giggle, in paw-some delight,
Making the critters join in on the night.

A raccoon in a top hat, a sight to behold,
Unleashes a routine that never gets old.
With a shimmy and shake, they scatter and flee,
As laughter erupts from the top of a tree.

Soon dawn breaks the fun, and off they will roam,
Leaving behind a well-ransacked home.
Yet in our hearts, there's a chuckle so bright,
For raccoon antics make everything right!

The Mischief of the Maple

A maple tree stands, with leaves all askew,
Covered in sap, it's the sticky debut.
The squirrels, they scamper with acorns galore,
Plotting a heist, oh, who could ask for more?

They bounce on the branches, they chatter and cheer,
Launching their acorns from far and near.
With each little thud, giggles bounce in the air,
It's a maple tree carnival, wild without care.

The branches, they quiver, in rhythm and rhyme,
As critters go flying, defying all time.
The birds join the fun, with a chirp and a tweet,
Why settle for nuts when you can dine on the fleet?

As day turns to dusk, they retreat with a grin,
Leaving the tulips to join in the din.
And the maple tree laughs, in its rustling way,
Knowing its mischief will brighten the day!

Jokes from the Big Ol' Oak

The big ol' oak tree, wise with age,
Sits in the yard, center stage.
With leaves that whisper, and branches so wide,
Tells jokes to the passers, with perfect pride.

"Why was the acorn so clever, you see?"
"It had a nutty idea, just like me!"
Punchlines delivered with rustling flair,
While squirrels gather, to laugh and to share.

A picnic of laughter beneath leafy spreads,
With giggles and snickers, the fun never ends.
Kids gather 'round, eyes bright with delight,
As the oak tells its tales on warm summer nights.

And when autumn arrives, the laughter won't cease,
For even the leaves dance with humor and peace.
The big ol' oak chuckles, a wise old sage,
For jokes shared in nature are never off-page!

Hilarity on the Homestead

On the farm lives a rooster who crows with a flair,
Waking the world with his raucous declare.
He struts round the yard in a most comical way,
Chasing the hens, just to join in the play.

The goats sneak a nibble of laundry hung high,
While the sheep share a laugh with the barn's old pie.
They bounce through the fields, with mischief in mind,
Creating a ruckus that's one of a kind.

The pig rolls in mud, then leaps with a squeal,
Trying to keep up with the whole farm's appeal.
Each creature partakes in the laughter and fun,
Under the bright shining warmth of the sun.

As dusk starts to settle, the laughter rings true,
With a chorus of critters, each one bids adieu.
Tomorrow they'll gather, with antics anew,
For life on the homestead is funny, it's true!

Quips from the Quaking Aspen

A tree once spoke with a wobbly tone,
'If I had legs, I'd dance all alone!'
The squirrels all chuckled, they giggled with glee,
'With roots like those, how funny you'd be!'

With branches a-sway and a soft, gentle shake,
It winked at the folks who would stop for a break.
'This bark's a joke, and the punchline, my leaves,
So stay for a laugh, don't grab your keys!'

As the wind played a tune through its foliage bright,
The Aspen stood proud, a hilarious sight.
It told silly tales of its youth on the hill,
As nature's own jest, it mastered the thrill!

Laughter in the Leaf Pile

In a mound of leaves, where the children would race,
A giggle erupted, splashing joy all over the place.
One leaf said, 'Hey, I'm wearing your shoe!'
'Well, that makes us both quite a funny crew!'

A hedgehog peeked out, with a grin on its face,
'This pile of leaves is my favorite place!'
With a rustle and tumble, they'd make such a scene,
A comedy show that would make all hearts glean.

And when autumn winds whispered a chortling tune,
The laughter rang clear, like a bright, silver moon.
Bits of humor fell softly with each swirling leaf,
In this jovial pile, there was no room for grief!

Misfit Mushrooms and Giggles Galore

Underneath the shady, gnarled oak tree,
A gathering of fungi was loud with esprit.
They joked about hats, how theirs weren't quite right,
'Yours looks like breakfast, mine's dinner tonight!'

One spoke, 'I once dreamed of a future so bright,
To dance in the sun, oh, what a delight!'
But every time he lifted his cap to glide,
He tripped on his stem, and fell with such pride!

They chuckled at stories of mushrooms who trip,
A hefty toadstool with a quippy quip.
Each echoed a snort as they rolled on the ground,
In this merry band, joy was always found!

The Funny Fungi Fable

Once in a glen, where the green grass grows tall,
Lived a bunch of shy mushrooms, afraid of it all.
They tried to make friends, but they couldn't agree,
On whether to giggle or just wait and see.

A wise old toad sat observing their plight,
'Tell a funny story, and you'll be all right!'
So they huddled together, shared tales one by one,
And soon they were roaring, oh, laughter was spun!

With jokes 'bout the rain and its puddly parade,
Each fungus grew bolder, no longer afraid.
The forest erupted in joy near the glade,
In the heart of the forest, friendship was made!

Laughter Lurks in the Larch

In the larch tree's embrace, a giggle's found,
Where branches sway and rustle all around.
A squirrel slips, a nut flies high,
And off it tumbles with a startled cry.

The woodpecker knocks with a rhythm so pure,
While the beavers scheme, making mischief for sure.
Leaves chuckle softly, the sun starts to beam,
In the woods, it's a laugh, or so it would seem.

A deer in a bowtie, oh what a sight!
Dancing in circles, under the moonlight.
Who knew the forest could be such a hoot?
With critters all dressed up, a grand soirée to boot!

Yet just when you think, it can't get more grand,
A raccoon's juggling acorns, its talent unplanned.
Laughter erupts from the crowd in this fun,
In the larch, joy blossoms, and worries are none.

Riddles from the Redwood Realm

In the redwood forest, a puzzle's at play,
With tree trunks whispering riddles each day.
A fox with spectacles and a brainy plan,
Ponders his riddle, a clever little man.

"Why did the acorn bring a suitcase around?"
The animals gathered, excitement profound.
"Cause it wanted to go visit the big oak tree!"
A chorus of laughter rang out with such glee.

An owl hooted wisely, perched up so high,
"Riddles are fun, but why let them fly?
Why not just ask the dandelions nearby?
They know every secret held deep in the sky!"

So under the branches, the riddles did soar,
With giggles and grins, oh, who could want more?
In the realm of redwoods, mischief's the key,
Where laughter grows wild, and all are set free.

Unexpected Humor in the Underbrush

In the underbrush thick, where shadows do play,
A hedgehog donned shades for his sunny display.
With a grin on his face, he roll-tumbles along,
In search of a friend to join in his song.

A rabbit with hiccups leaps over a log,
Chasing a butterfly, a comical cog.
"Did you hear the last joke from that clever old fox?
It was more twisted than all of our socks!"

The chipmunks were giggling, providing the beat,
As the underbrush teemed with whimsical feet.
Even the mushrooms seemed ready to dance,
With their caps bobbing up in a jolly romance.

So if you stroll through this thicket of cheer,
Just watch for the antics that bubble up near.
For humor hides here, in shadows and light,
Where laughter erupts, and troubles take flight.

Squirrel Shenanigans in the Sycamore

In the sycamore tree, mischief's the game,
A squirrel named Nutty had made quite the name.
With acorns like marbles, he rolled them with flair,
Challenging friends with a playful dare!

He raced with a rabbit, both swift on their toes,
While pigeons cooed softly, they all watched the show.
"Who'll make the best leap from the branch to the ground?"
With a gasp from the crowd, the winner was found!

Nutty then donned a tiny little hat,
Waving to onlookers, just fancy that!
The sparrows applauded, and the branches would sway,
As laughter erupted in a comedic way.

With squirrels and critters all gathered around,
In sycamore shade, hilarity's found.
So if you find fun in a world that does snicker,
Join Nutty the squirrel, for laughter's the kicker!

Jolly Journeys Through the Grove

With boots made for stomping, they dance on the trail,
Chasing after shadows, they giggle and wail.
A wide-eyed raccoon joins the frolicsome pack,
Throwing acorns in jest and never looking back.

Through sun-dappled paths, they prance with delight,
While the trees sway and chuckle under moonlight.
A bird's silly whistle makes everyone pause,
As branches break laughter and cheer without cause.

Pine needles bounce high like confetti on air,
Each twist and each turn, they find joy everywhere.
They tumble through thickets, all scrapes turned to glee,
In the heart of the forest, wild spirits run free.

With the scent of fresh pine and a breeze that won't quit,
These jolly escapades are quite a hit!
They'll return to the grove, for the fun never ends,
Bringing laughter and stories, with all of their friends.

Lighthearted Lore of the Lake

At the edge of the water, a duck has a plan,
To waddle and quack, like a jovial man.
The splashes of fish, they dance in delight,
While frogs join the chorus, all day and all night.

A turtle in shades, sunbathing with flair,
Yet slips off his log, creating a scare.
With a plop and a splash, laughter echoes the shore,
As friends rally 'round, asking, "Can we do more?"

The sun sets like candy, a swirl of bright hues,
As the stars start to twinkle, sharing silly views.
Each tale that they spin makes the moonbeam beam bright,
With a chuckle or two, they bask in the night.

From lore of the lake, they emerge with a grin,
With quips and with giggles, it's always a win!
For in these merry moments, hearts flourish and swell,
Creating pure joy that no one can quell.

Chuckling Under the Canopy

In the shade of tall trees, the critters convene,
Where a squirrel tells tales, and they can hardly breathe.
A wise old owl, with a glint in his eye,
Woos the crowd with a pun, oh my, oh my!

With branches swaying, the laughter takes flight,
A raccoon makes faces, a comical sight.
The chatter's contagious, a melody sweet,
As shadows grow longer, they jive to the beat.

Each chirp of a bird adds a note to the fun,
Creating a symphony till daylight is done.
"More snacks!" cries a hedgehog, with gusto so grand,
While the squirrels exchange nuts with a flourish and band.

As twilight encroaches, their giggles persist,
With the thrill of their antics, who could resist?
Under leafy green roofs, they'll never grow old,
For laughs shared together are purest of gold.

Sassy Squirrels and Snickering Stumps

Sassy squirrels scamper, their tails in the air,
Daring each other to leap without care.
With a wiggle and tease, they plot quite the show,
As snickering stumps watch, giggling below.

One squirrel dressed stylish, in snazzy old shoes,
Claiming he's king of the forest, with grand news.
They challenge his crown with a game of charades,
Unraveling laughter in the sun's golden glades.

A chilly breeze sweeps in, but fun doesn't fade,
They form a grand circle, a dance that won't trade.
The tree trunks are joining, their roots start to sway,
Amidst snickers and chortles, they frolic and play.

So here's to the mischief, the giggles, the cheer,
In the heart of the forest, all worries disappear.
For sassy days spent by stumps full of laughs,
Are the moments that bring joy to the life's many paths.

The Eclectic Elm Encounter

In a meadow of quirks, they stood so tall,
Three elms, with plans, to have a ball.
One wore a hat, another some shoes,
The last had a mustache, a sight to amuse.

They danced in the breeze, a sight to behold,
The branches swaying, like stories retold.
One tripped on a root, went tumbling around,
Now that tree giggles every time it's found.

They threw a grand party beneath the bright moon,
With acorn confetti, and a squirrel cartoon.
Invited the critters to dance and prance,
The owls brought the snacks, giving all a chance.

With laughter as music, it echoed the night,
These elms knew the secret – to make joy take flight.
So if you wander past their gleeful domain,
Join in the fun, and you'll feel the same.

Wacky Woodland Wanderings

Through the woods with a skip, I chanced to trod,
Circus critters danced, with a leap and nod.
A raccoon in tights was flipping upside down,
While a hedgehog juggled, wearing a crown.

The owls were judges, in robes made of leaves,
Declaring wild talent, as everyone believes.
The fox played the flute, in a jazzy delight,
While the frogs croaked the beat all through the night.

Squirrels spun tales, taller than the trees,
Of acorns as treasure, and pirate's grand fees.
The chipmunks were pirates, with patches and swords,
In search of the treasure, they gobbled the cords.

But as dawn approached, the fun had to cease,
Yet the woods kept the laughter, a treasure of peace.
Next time you wander, keep your spirit bright,
For wacky adventures await day and night.

Rambunctious Root Riddles

Oh, wiggly roots, all tangled and tight,
Every pathway they make is a riddle of light.
One asked a question, a mystery grand,
"Why don't trees check their watches for sand?"

With giggles that echoed, the forest replied,
"Because time is a tree's most whimsical ride!"
They chuckled and danced, as shadows grew long,
Their banter a melody, nature's own song.

A tangle of vines introduced a new game,
A race through the thickets, to glory and fame.
But one little sprout, with roots all askew,
Started tumbling down, like it hardly knew!

The punchline was simple, no need for a kick,
The forest erupted, a joke that would stick.
So wander through roots, and join in the fun,
For laughter's the sunlight, where riddles are spun.

The Cheeky Cherries' Eccentricity

High up in the tree, where the sunshine beams,
Sat cherries in hats, with most daring dreams.
One dreamed of dancing, another of flight,
While the cheekiest one sang all through the night.

"Why wear a hat?" asked a wise little bee,
"To keep out the sun, and be fancy like me!"
The cherries all giggled, vibrating with cheer,
As they plotted a party, to celebrate here.

The breeze brought a twirl, and invited a breeze,
The cherries made cupcakes and dressed up the leaves.
With sprinkles and laughter, they filled up the sky,
While the nearby squirrels let out a shriek and a sigh.

So if you find cherries with mirth in their eyes,
Join their little gathering beneath the blue skies.
For laughter is sweetest, just like their bright hue,
In the orchard of joy, where the fun's always new.

The Treehouse of Tiny Jokes

Up in the branches, where sunlight gleams,
Lies a treehouse filled with giggly dreams.
Squirrels and owls share riddles galore,
Each punchline brings laughter that begs for more.

One swing of the door, and out bursts a pun,
The forest erupts—oh, what fun!
A worm in a suit, he dances with glee,
Telling tall tales about the old tree.

Leaves whisper laughter, it's a chuckle parade,
Each critter in line has a joke to be made.
From acorns with quirks to pinecone pranks,
In this lively house, there's no room for thanks.

So if you feel down, or the day seems gray,
Climb up to the treetops, come join the play.
Bring all your giggles, and leave woes behind,
In the house of small jokes, good times you'll find!

How to Avoid a Porcupine Prick

Out in the woods where the quirks roam free,
Lives a prickly fellow, quite hard to see.
With quills like arrows, he's not one to hug,
So here's how to skip that porcupine slug.

Step lightly and softly, be quiet as air,
Look for his laugh, it's prickly but fair.
If you catch him snickering, you best turn around,
Before you embrace him, take heed of the sound.

Avoid in tight spaces, don't trip on a root,
Watch out for sharp things—it's quite absolute.
Offer a joke that makes him turn pale,
And quickly retreat before you turn frail.

When walking in woods, keep your eyes peeled wide,
A grin on your face, and a tell-tale guide.
For if you can chuckle at his crafty quirk,
You may just escape the prickly work!

Tumbles and Treetops

In the high branches, the children play,
Swinging and laughing through bright sunny days.
A tumble, a roll, laughter fills the air,
Each trip sends out giggles, without a care.

They climb to the skies, then slide down with glee,
Turning backflips like squirrels in a spree.
A splash in the mud? A triumphant cheer!
In this circus of trees, there's nothing to fear.

Branches sway gently, like a comedic dance,
While tree frogs join in with their nature romance.
With every loud thud, there's laughter galore,
The treetops are bouncing, begging for more.

So take off your shoes and feel the cool breeze,
Join in the antics with the rustling leaves.
For tumbling in treetops is a glorious game,
Let's play until sunset, all wild and untame!

The Wildflower Laughingstock

In a field of wildflowers, laughter takes flight,
Each blossom's a joker, a colorful sight.
The daisies gossip with petals all spry,
While dandelions dance in the soft, sunny sky.

A sunflower winks, with a grin oh-so-wide,
He tickles the bees that bounce by his side.
With jokes in the breeze, they all play their part,
For laughter is nature's most beautiful art.

The bees buzz a tune, in a funny parade,
While grasshoppers hop with their jokes well displayed.
Amidst laughing petals, the grass joins along,
In the choir of giggles, they all sing their song.

So if you feel dull, just stroll through this patch,
Let flowers remind you, that humor can hatch.
In fields of wild dreams, find joy in the stock,
For life's just a jest—be the laughingstock!

The Tall Tale Teak

In a forest so grand, where tall trees do sway,
There lived a teak with a lot to say.
He spun stories of clouds that could dance on the ground,
And of squirrels that sang, oh what a sound!

His bark would laugh, his leaves would crack,
As he claimed he once rode a bear on its back.
The other trees chuckled, they thought it absurd,
But the teak just grinned, with a wink and a spurred.

One day came a breeze that tossed him around,
He tangled with vines and fell to the ground.
With twigs all a-twist, he laughed with glee,
"Now I'm just a funny old tree, can't you see?"

And so in the woods, he's the favorite fellow,
With tales so absurd, they're truly quite mellow.
While other trees stand, all stoic and tight,
The teak keeps us laughing, a magnificent sight.

Sassy Saplings and Snickers

In a plot of young trees, full of life and sass,
The saplings would gossip as the seasons would pass.
Their leaves flickered bright, from green to a spree,
Chasing shadows of giggles, wild and free.

"Oh, did you see? That old oak's lost a limb!"
Squeaked a little pine, with laughter so grim.
"And the birch? She tripped over her roots once or twice,
Fell down like a feather, oh wasn't it nice?"

These saplings, so cheeky, would poke fun on a whim,
Daring the others to join in, on a limb.
Each breeze brought a snicker, a poke in the bark,
As they whispered sweet nothings till it was dark.

In their garden of giggles, life was a game,
Each joke brought them closer, no one felt lame.
So if you wander there, with a smile on your face,
You may find yourself tangled in their playful race.

Giddy Gardens of Giggleweed

In gardens so bright, where giggleweed grows,
The flowers would chuckle, as everyone knows.
With petals that danced in the warm summer air,
They tickled the noses of folks passing there.

"Oh, look at that bee with a wobble and sway!"
Said a dandelion, laughing all day.
"It buzzes like it's had too much nectar to sip,
And nearly collided with that sunny red lip!"

The tulips all quaked with a shimmering cheer,
As the frogs croaked along, spreading joy far and near.
The sunlight would shimmer, the laughter would bloom,
In that garden of giggles, all worries would zoom.

When shadows grew long, and night came to play,
The stars would join in, in their twinkly ballet.
For every bright flower in that jolly spread,
Held a secret of laughter, where joy never fled.

The Blundering Birch Brigade

In a grove of birches, clumsy and spry,
The brigade of blunders reached up to the sky.
With branches a-flail, they stumbled about,
Causing ruckus and rainbows, when they whirled out.

"Oh dear!" cried the one with the bark of pure white,
"I just tripped on my roots in broad daylight!"
The others would giggle, just losing their grace,
As one fell to the side, with a chuckle on his face.

They took turns at weaving a wobbly dance,
In a flurry of leaves, their luck was askance.
Each twist was a tumble, each sway was a shout,
In the blundering birch brigade, joy never sprouted.

Yet when moonbeams shone and the night glowed bright,

Their laughter would echo, a whimsical sight.
So if you stroll by, and you hear a loud cheer,
Know it's the birches, spreading happiness near.

The Peculiar Pecan Parade

Pecans in tuxedos, waltzing down the lane,
Chanting silly songs, making quite a gain.
The squirrels in bowties, tipping their hats,
Joining in the fun with their jolly chats.

A nutty conductor waves a golden wand,
While the acorns all dance in a leafy band.
The crowd is a mix of critters galore,
Laughing and cheering, always wanting more.

A pecan drops low, does a somersault spin,
Followed by a walnut with a goofy grin.
The whole tree giggles, swaying with delight,
As twilight descends, they party all night.

When morning arrives, the parade takes a bow,
With nuts full of laughter, tastes just like chow.
So next time you see a pecan parade,
Join in on the fun, it's the best escapade!

Chuckles Under the Cherry Tree

Underneath the cherry, the laughter takes flight,
Birds are sharing jokes, what a funny sight!
The blossoms all giggle, petals turn pink,
As bees buzz along, giving us a wink.

A chubby young robin tried to tell a joke,
But tripped on a twig and started to choke.
The cherries burst out in a raucous cheer,
As the shadow of a cat quietly creeps near.

Then a wise old owl perched up in a nook,
Said, "Life's like a cherry, just take a good look!"
With laughter and sweetness, we all found our glee,
Beneath that jolly, joy-filled cherry tree.

So remember the laughter, as life tries to tease,
With friends and ripe cherries, we'll handle with ease.
Every chuckle we share brings us closer, you see,
In the shade of the branches, so wild and so free.

Juggling Jays and Quirky Quips

Jays in bright colors juggling shiny stones,
Cracking up each other with their funny tones.
One drops a pebble, oh what a big splash,
And the crowd bursts out laughing, what a hearty crash!

With wings flapping wildly, they tumble and roll,
Chasing after giggles, their ultimate goal.
A jay took a bow, then slipped on a leaf,
Balance lost in laughter, oh what a relief!

They play tag with shadows, their antics a thrill,
Poking fun at each other, laughter to spill.
With each quirky quip, their bond only grows,
In frolicsome flight, the joy overflows.

As twilight descends, they gather in twos,
Swapping tales of blunders and the silliest views.
So if you're feeling blue, find a jay for a chat,
For juggling together is where laughter's at!

The Comedic Chestnut Chronicles

Once in the forest, a chestnut did claim,
"I'm the funniest nut, now isn't that fame?"
With a witty little grin, he started to jest,
While all of his friends laughed and squashed their unrest.

A wise old oak chuckled from high up above,
"Share your quirks, dear chestnut, it's laughter we love!"
So he spun silly stories about Mr. Acorn,
Whose hat was too big and made him forlorn.

Nutty shenanigans brought giggles galore,
As the chestnut danced, they begged him for more.
"What's round on the outside and funny within?"
He paused for a moment, then shouted, "A grin!"

The trees swayed in rhythm, a comedic encore,
As night fell upon them, laughter soared and roared.
In the chronicles of chestnuts, a lesson rings true:
Joy shared together is the best thing to do!

www.ingramcontent.com/pod-product-compliance
Lightning Source LLC
Chambersburg PA
CBHW071834160426
43209CB00003B/288